Draw It!

Cars

Patricia Walsh
Illustrations by David Westerfield

Heinemann Library
Chicago, Illinois

©2001 Reed Educational & Professional Publishing
Published by Heinemann Library,
an imprint of Reed Educational & Professional Publishing,
Chicago, Illinois

Customer Service 888-454-2279

Visit our website at www.heinemannlibrary.com

Designed by Meighan Depke
Illustrated by David Westerfield
Photos by Kim Saar
Printed in Hong Kong

05 04 03 02 01
10 9 8 7 6 5 4 3

Library of Congress Cataloging-in-Publication Data
Walsh, Patricia, 1951-
     Cars / by Patricia Walsh ; illustrations by David Westerfield.
        p. cm. – (Draw it!)
     Includes bibliographical references and index.
     Summary: Instructions and illustrations demonstrate how to draw various motorized
vehicles, including the Ford Model T, Chevy Bel Air, Corvette, Volkswagen Beetle, and
     Hummer.
     ISBN 1-57572-348-4
     1. Automobiles in art—Juvenile literature. 2. Drawing—Technique—Juvenile literature.
     [1. Automobiles in art. 2. Drawing—Technique.] I. Westerfield, David, 1956- ill. II. Title.

NC825.A8W35 2000
743'.89629222—dc21

                                    00-023386

Some words are shown in bold, **like this.** You can
find out what they mean by looking in the glossary.

Contents

Introduction...4

Ford Model T...6

Chevy Bel Air..8

Stock Car...10

Formula One Car.................................12

Funny Car...14

Dragster 16

Dune Buggy 18

Corvette 20

Porsche Boxster 22

Jeep Grand Cherokee..........................24

Volkswagen New Beetle 26

Hummer 28

Glossary...*30*

Art Glossary...*31*

More Books *32*

Index...*32*

Introduction

Would you like to improve the pictures that you draw?

Well, you can! In this book, the artist has drawn some favorite cars. He has used lines and shapes to draw each picture in small, simple steps. Follow these steps and your picture will come together for you too.

Here is advice from the artist:

- Always draw lightly at first.

- Draw all the shapes and pieces in the right places.

- Pay attention to the spaces between the lines as well as the lines themselves.

- Add details and **shading** to finish your drawing.

- And finally, erase the lines you don't need.

You only need a few supplies to get started.

There are just four things you need for drawing:

- a pencil (medium or soft). You might also use a fine marker or pen to finish your drawing.
- a pencil sharpener
- paper
- an eraser—a **kneaded eraser** works best. It can be squeezed into small or odd shapes. This eraser can also make pencil lines lighter without erasing them.

Now, are you ready? Do you have everything?
Then turn the page and let's draw!

*The drawings in this book were done by David Westerfield. David started drawing when he was very young. In college, he studied drawing and painting. Now he is a **commercial artist** who owns his own graphic design business. He has two children, and he likes to draw with them. David's advice to anyone who hopes to become an artist is, "practice, practice, practice—and learn as much as you can from other artists."*

Draw a Ford Model T

In 1908 Henry Ford began building the Model T. It was a simple car that people could afford. From 1908 until 1927, The Ford Motor Company made more than 15 million Model Ts on the first automobile assembly line.

1 **Sketch** a box shape for the body. Use a **straightedge** to make straight lines.

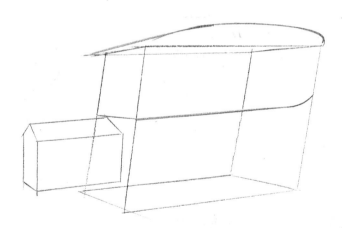

2 Add a smaller box with a tent-shape to the front. This is the hood. Add a curved line to the top of the body. Divide the body in half with a straight line.

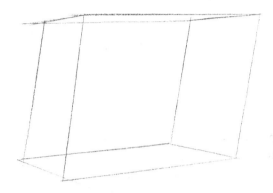

3 Use a straightedge to draw four short **guidelines** below the car. Then draw two rings on this side of the car and two incomplete rings on the other side of the car. These are the wheels. They should just touch the guidelines.

4 Draw curved lines over the wheels. Connect the curves on this side with a double line. Add oval headlights to the front. Draw six **parallel** lines on the side of the hood. Draw two rectangles with rounded corners on the side for doors.

5 Draw the tops of the front and back seats. Draw short lines on the seats to make the cushions. Divide the front windshield with two **horizontal** lines. Add a stick and oval for the steering wheel. In back, add two Y-shaped roof supports and two small square windows.

6 Draw a small circle in the center of each wheel and straight lines from each circle to the tire. Darken the important lines. Add **shading.** The 1923 Model T is black because that was the only color it came in.

Draw a Chevy Bel Air

In 1957, the Chevy Bel Air was "sweet, smooth, and sassy." Chevrolet's two-door **convertible** cost $2,511, and Chevrolet sold 47,562 of them. Today people who collect **classic** cars think a '57 Chevy is the car to have.

1 **Sketch guidelines** to make a rectangular box for the body. Use a **straightedge** to make your lines straight.

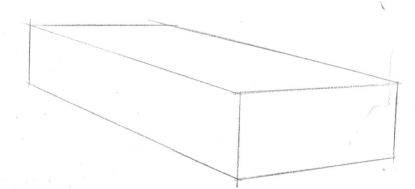

2 Use gently curving lines to draw the windshield on top of the body. Draw two half-circles on the side for **wheel wells**.

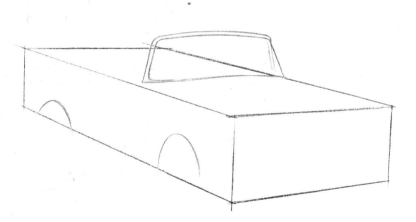

3 On the front, draw a circle on each corner for headlights. Draw two long ovals, one inside the other, for the front **grille.** Add a rectangle for the license plate and four small circles to the center oval. Add two long lines from the windshield to the grille. Shape the tail fin at the rear with a slightly curved line.

4 Draw two wheels in the wheel wells. Divide the top of the body with three lines behind the windshield to make the front and back seats. Just behind the windshield, draw a half-oval for the **dashboard.** Behind it, add part of a circle for the steering wheel.

5 Make the tail fin lines bolder. Add two pointed hood ornaments and a V-shaped **insignia** to the front. Add a triangle and straight line to the side of the car for a **chrome** strip and lines for the door and handle to the side. Draw a circle for the side mirror. Finish the windshield with lines for visors, a rectangle for a side window vent, and a small rectangle in the middle for a rearview mirror.

6 Erase the body guidelines you no longer need. Add a license plate number. **Shade** the car, leaving a bit of white to make the car gleam. Shade a shadow under the car.

Draw a Stock Car

NASCAR stock car racing is the most popular auto racing in the United States. A stock car looks like a regular passenger car, but under the hood is a powerful engine. Stock cars race on oval tracks and reach speeds of 200 miles (322 kilometers) per hour.

1 **Sketch** a rectangular box, but slant the front of the box downward. Use a **straightedge** to draw straight lines. Draw two lines across the front.

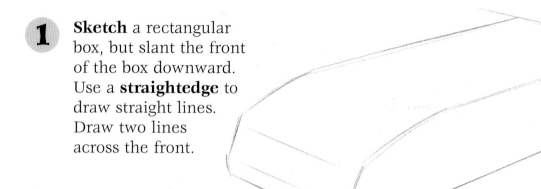

2 Add a tent-shaped roof to the box using three four-sided shapes.

3 Draw a circle inside a circle for each wheel on the side. Darken the curved line to make **wheel wells**.

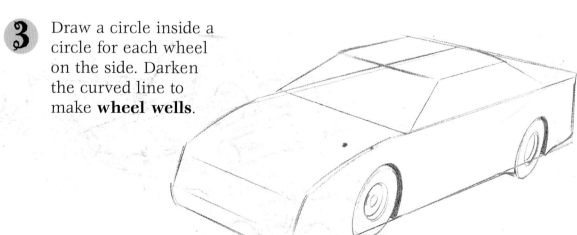

4 Draw five rectangles on the slanted front to show the **grille** and headlights.

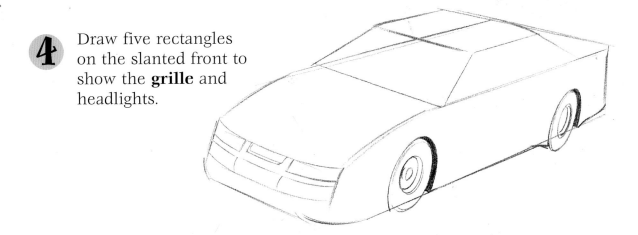

5 Draw a straight line on each side of the windshield. Use **crosshatching** for the driver's side window net. Add a triangle for the side window. Draw a short line at the back of the car.

6 **Shade** the front and side windows. Add a big number to the roof and side. Draw the **logos** of your car's sponsors. Make straight, soft pencil strokes behind the car to show that it is moving. Shade a shadow under the car.

Draw a Formula One Car

Formula One racing cars are the most expensive racing cars. They are built to a formula that tells the car builders what the size and weight of the cars must be.

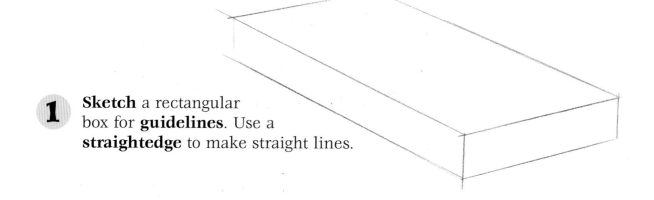

1 **Sketch** a rectangular box for **guidelines**. Use a **straightedge** to make straight lines.

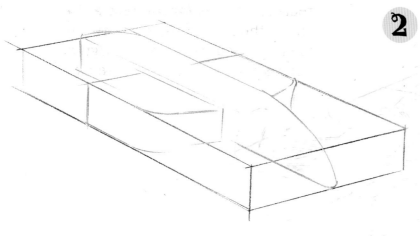

2 Sketch a banana-shape through the center of the box for the main body of the car. Make the car wider in the middle with straight and curved lines.

3 Scoop out an open **cockpit** for the driver by drawing an oval with pointed ends in the center. Draw a wide upside-down V for the **roll bar** behind the cockpit. Add curved and straight lines on each side of the car at the rear.

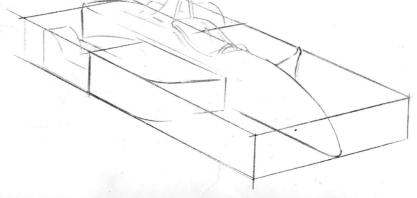

4 Draw two wheels at the rear of the car and one on each side at the front. Make the rear wheels wider than the front wheels. Connect the wheels to the main body by drawing pairs of straight lines from the tires to the main body.

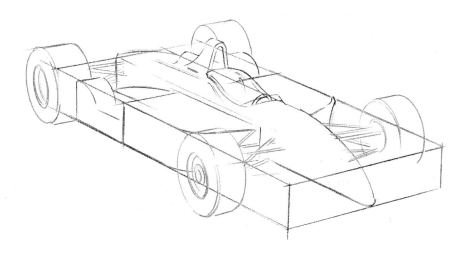

5 Add front and rear **airfoils**. Draw a rectangular box for the rear airfoil above the rear of the car. Use rows of small rectangles and triangular shapes for the airfoils on the front.

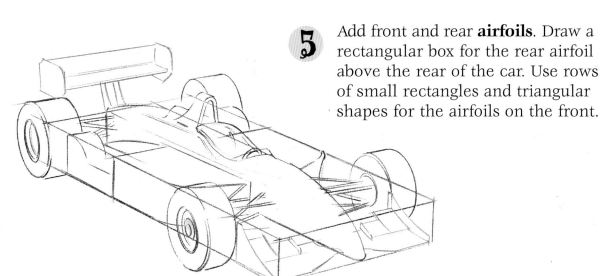

6 **Shade** the body of the car. Add a number on the front, and draw the **logos** of the racing team's sponsors. Shade a shadow underneath the car.

Draw a Funny Car

A Funny Car is a car used in **drag racing**. It looks like a passenger car, but it is much faster and more powerful. Some Funny Cars go from 0 to 100 miles (0 to 161 kilometers) per hour in less than 1 second.

1 **Sketch** a rectangular box. Make it curve at the rear.

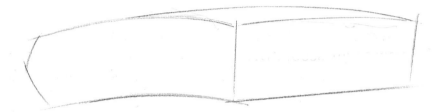

2 Draw **parallel** lines to add the slightly rounded roof. Draw the side window and windshield using four-sided shapes. Draw a long double-lined oval on the front for the **grille**.

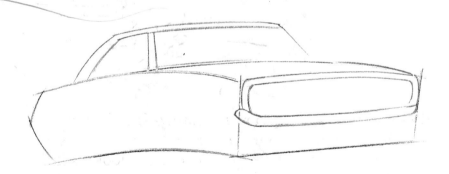

3 Draw deep curves on the side for **wheel wells**. Round off the bottom line on the front end. Add a small triangle-shape to the rear to make the **spoiler**.

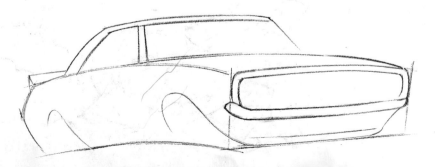

4 Add the wide tires. Draw only part of the far wheels. Draw wavy lines between the wheels to make the underside of the car.

5 Draw a rectangle with three tiny circles on the hood for the engine air scoop. Draw two short lines from the scoop to the grille and two round headlights on the grille. Add straight lines across the grille and two smaller circles below the grille. Add four short tube shapes to the side for exhaust pipes.

6 Add two lines for the door, a number, and the sponsors' logos on the side. **Shade** the car and the tires. Then shade a shadow under the car to make it look as if the front tires are off the ground. Give your Funny Car a nickname and write it on the side.

Draw a Dragster

Drag racing is a high-speed event. Dragsters race two at a time on a straight, quarter-mile (0.4 kilometer) track called a drag strip. A race can finish in five seconds! At the end of the race, parachutes on the rear of the cars open to slow them down.

1 Draw a long, narrow triangle. Use a **straightedge** to make the lines straight.

2 Draw four **vertical** lines and two **horizontal** lines above the triangle to begin the back **spoiler**. Draw two curved lines on the front point.

3 Draw circles to make a thick back wheel at the left side. Draw only part of a wheel on the right side. **Sketch** ovals for the small front wheels. Draw two **parallel** lines across the front wheels. Add a triangle to each end of the lines to make the front spoiler.

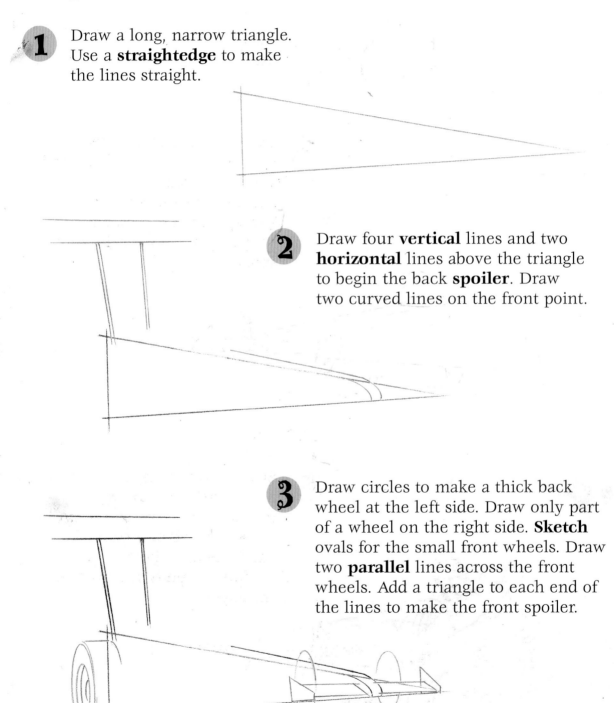

4 Draw an oval and short, straight lines inside each front wheel. Then draw two U-shaped **roll bars** over the center of the car. Connect the open ends of the Us with short straight lines.

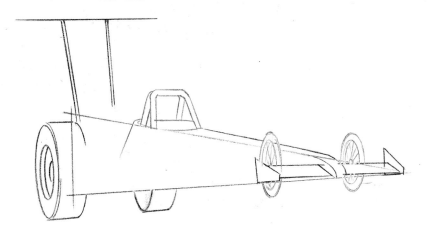

5 Use rows of circles, ovals, and tube shapes to draw the engine behind the roll bars. Draw an X between the support bars of the rear spoiler. Add a four-sided shape to each end of the rear spoiler.

6 **Shade** the wheels and the body and shade a shadow under the car. Add a sponsor's **logo** to the side. Show clouds of smoke behind the dragster by drawing puffs and shading the edges.

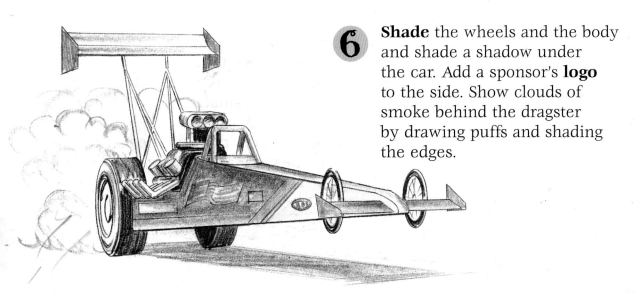

Draw a Dune Buggy

Dune buggies race on dirt race tracks. The track has straightaways, turns, jumps, bumps, and a water hole. Dune buggies go fast, brake suddenly, and make quick turns. It takes a good driver to keep the car in the race.

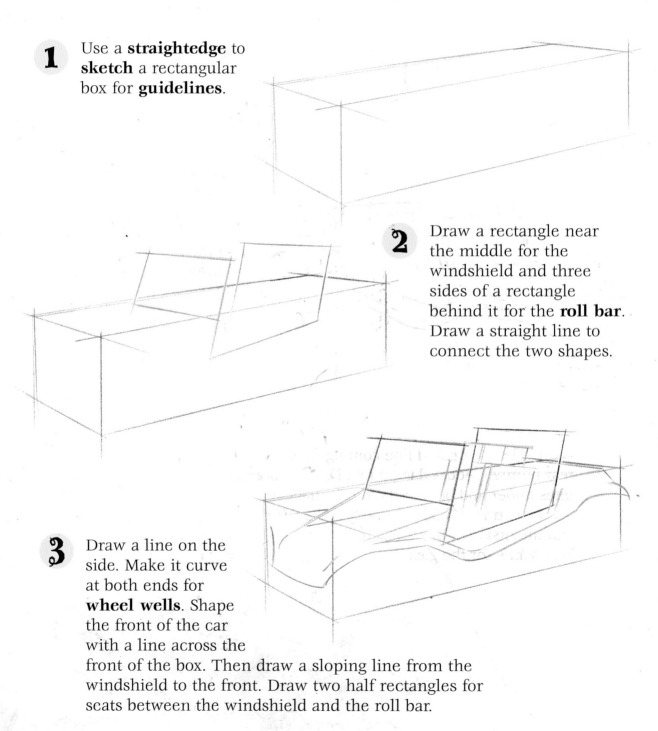

1 Use a **straightedge** to **sketch** a rectangular box for **guidelines**.

2 Draw a rectangle near the middle for the windshield and three sides of a rectangle behind it for the **roll bar**. Draw a straight line to connect the two shapes.

3 Draw a line on the side. Make it curve at both ends for **wheel wells**. Shape the front of the car with a line across the front of the box. Then draw a sloping line from the windshield to the front. Draw two half rectangles for scats between the windshield and the roll bar.

4 Add two curved lines to the front for the bumper. Draw an oval and a half circle to make headlights on the hood. Add a large rectangle inside the windshield and a second line to the roll bar. Add half a rectangle to the rear.

5 Draw ovals to make the two wheels that can be seen in this picture and connect them to each other with a straight line. Erase the guidelines.

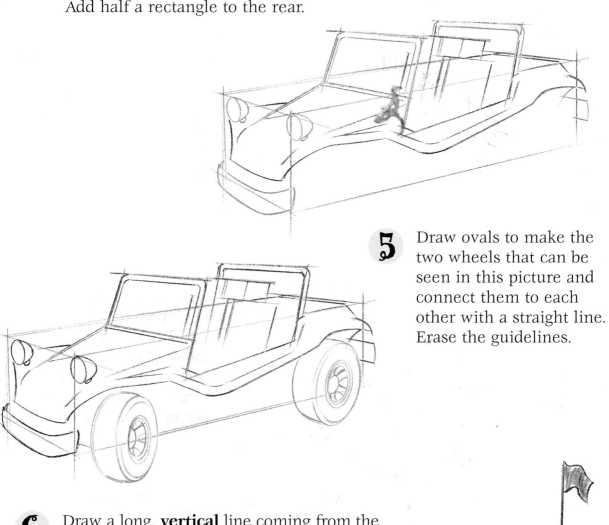

6 Draw a long, **vertical** line coming from the rear bumper. Add a flag on top. Draw swooping lines under and behind the dune buggy to show the track. Shade the body, seats, tires, and underside of the car. Leave a little white for the gleam.

Draw a Corvette

The Corvette was the first American sports car. Today lovers of old and new Corvettes—like this 2000 model—join clubs and share information on the Internet. They also visit the National Corvette Museum in Kentucky.

1 Use a **straightedge** to draw a rectangular **guideline** that has a top line angling downward. Draw a guideline for the ground near the underside of the car.

2 Draw two circles on the side for wheels. The wheels should touch the ground line. Add a small circle in the center of each wheel. Use three straight lines for the roof.

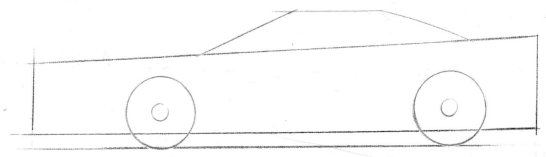

3 Draw the body of the car using a sloping line to shape the front and rounded corners at the rear. Draw deep curves over the wheels for **wheel wells.**

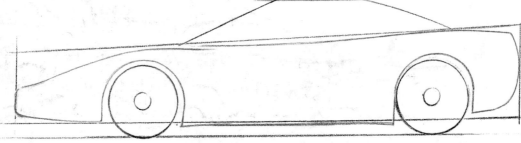

4 Draw a second line for the hood and trunk. Add the windows by drawing two four-sided shapes and a triangle under the roof line.

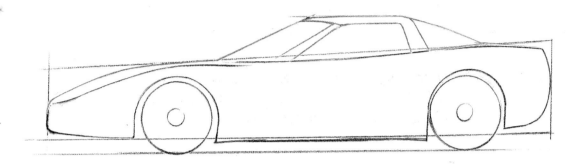

5 Draw a circle and a star-shape inside each wheel. Add a small oval on the side for a mirror. Draw two upside-down U-shapes in the side window for the tops of the seats. Add two curved lines under the car for the two far wheels.

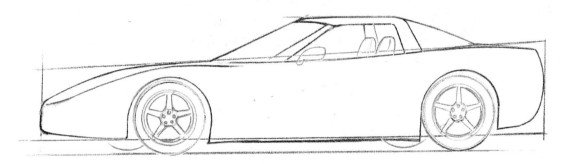

6 Draw door lines and a door handle on the side. Add a short line and a **horizontal** line behind the front wheel to give the car style. **Shade** the car and add a thin shadow underneath.

Draw a Porsche Boxster

The Porsche Boxster was first seen at the 1993 Detroit Auto Show and first sold to sports car lovers in 1997. Its name comes from two words: boxer, the name of its engine, and Speedster, a popular car Porsche used to make.

1 Start with two long ovals, one on top of the other, to make **guidelines**.

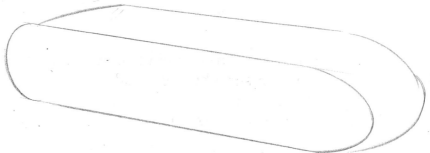

2 Add a four-sided shape in the middle for the windshield. Draw a C-shape on top of the ovals to begin the interior.

3 Draw circles for wheels. Make a curved line above each circle for the **wheel wells.** Draw half of each wheel above the bottom of the car.

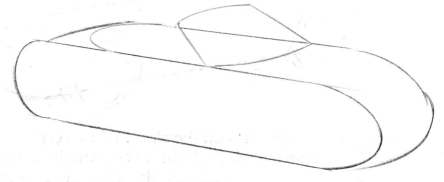

4 Draw a second line along the windshield. Draw an oval in the middle for the side mirror. Shape the hood and headlights by drawing two straight lines with loops at the ends. Add three curved lines for the front **grille.**

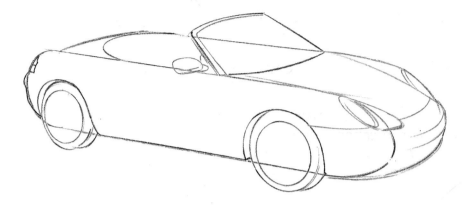

5 Use upside-down U-shapes to add two seats and two **roll bars.** Connect them with straight lines. Add a small oval to the center of the windshield for the rearview mirror. Add a straight and curved line for the **dash.** Draw part of a circle for the steering wheel.

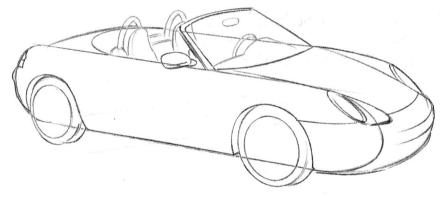

6 Draw curved door lines on the side. Add two C-shapes for the side vent and small ovals for a door handle and gas tank door. Draw C-shapes inside the wheels to show the spokes. **Shade** in the shapes and leave the spokes white. Sharpen details with shading. Add a shadow under the car.

Draw a Jeep Grand Cherokee

The name Jeep comes from the letters GP. They stood for General Purpose World War II military vehicle. Today's Jeep Grand Cherokee is nothing like an Army jeep. It has room for five people and a place to plug in a computer.

1 Use a **straightedge** to **sketch** a rectangular **guideline**. Add a straight line below for a ground line.

2 Draw the top with two slanted lines connected by a straight line. Use angled lines to clip off the front and lower corners.

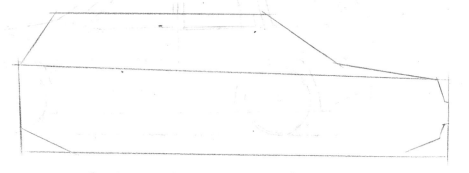

3 Divide the guideline rectangle with a **horizontal** line. Draw two deep curves on the side for **wheel wells**. Draw two circles for tires under the wheel wells. The wheels should just touch the ground line. Make a plus-sign in each wheel for guidelines.

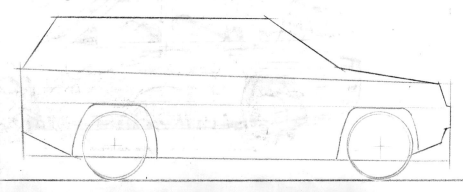

4 Draw **parallel** lines that curve down at the ends for a roof rack. Use four-sided shapes to draw three side windows and a windshield. Draw a small oval in the corner of the front side window to add a side mirror.

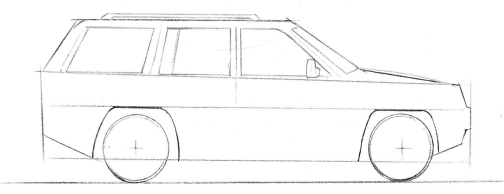

5 Draw horizontal lines that curve over each wheel. Draw parallel lines below to add side trim. Add a rectangular taillight to the rear and a headlight to the front.

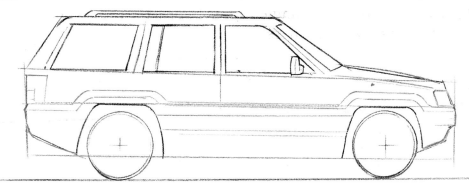

6 Add a star shape to the center of each wheel. **Shade** the wheel wells, tires, and body. Shade the windows, but leave some white to make them look like glass. Add a little shading to the ground line under the car.

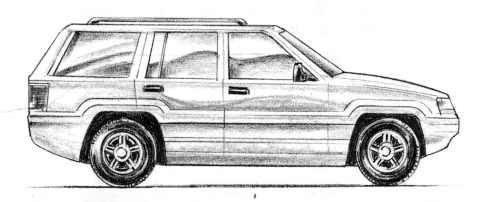

Draw a Volkswagen New Beetle

The Germans first made the Volkswagen more than 60 years ago. Someone said it looked like a beetle, and the name stuck. The New Beetle was introduced in 1998. Its shape is similar to the old Beetle, but it is a modern car.

1 Use a **straightedge** to draw **guidelines** for the ground, underside of the car, and bottom of the windows.

2 Connect the top two lines with a line that curves downward in front and a line that comes to a point at the rear. Draw a curved dome for the roof.

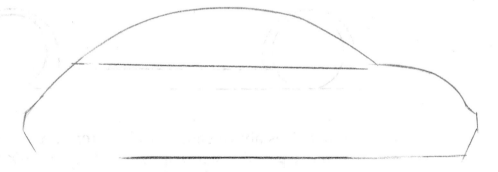

3 Draw two circles that are mostly above the underside of the car for wheels. The wheels should just touch the ground line. Add a curved line over each wheel for **wheel wells**.

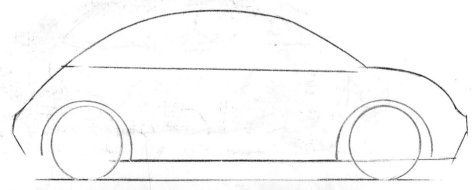

4 Draw a curved line under the roof line. Add three **vertical** lines near the center. The lines should go from the roof line to the window guideline.

5 Draw small rectangular shapes to add bumper details to the front and rear. Draw an oval on the nose for a headlight. Draw half a circle for a side mirror and an oval for a door handle.

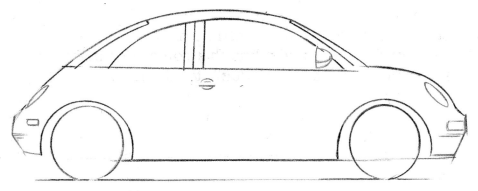

6 Draw long curved lines above each wheel for **fenders**. Add door lines and the top of the steering wheel above the door. Finish the wheels with little half-circles around a center circle. **Shade** the insides of the car, the wheels, and the ground line under the car.

Draw a Hummer

The first Hummers were U.S. Army **HUMVEEs**. In the late 1970s, they began carrying soldiers and equipment through snow, sand, water, and mud. Today's Hummers have stereo systems and leather seats and are not just for the military.

1 Use a **straightedge** to draw **guidelines** of a large box with a smaller box on top.

2 Draw curved lines on the side of the bottom box for **wheel wells**. Divide the front with a straight line. Add a rectangle below that line.

3 Draw two rectangles for front windows and two squares for side windows. Use straight lines to show the doors. Round the corners of the top box to make the roof.

4 Draw ovals for the three thick tires that can be seen. Connect the front wheels to the front rectangle with straight lines. Draw two short lines under the front corner and fill the space with short **horizontal** lines.

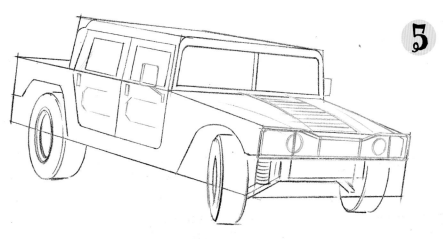

5 Add door handles and a square side mirror. Draw two large Cs on the doors. Add two sets of **parallel** lines to the hood and fill the space between with horizontal lines. Draw a bow tie shape on the front and put two circles on it for headlights. Erase the guidelines.

6 Add **tread** lines to the tires and a square bumper behind the left rear wheel. Use dark shading for the tires and the underside of the vehicle's body. Lightly shade the windows and body. Leave a little white to show the glass. Add large rocks and a shadow under the vehicle.

Glossary

airfoil wing-like surface that helps to control a vehicle by pressing a car to the road, allowing it to go faster in the turns

chrome chromium, a shiny metal

classic model or guide for others like it; car that is more than twenty years old

cockpit place where the driver sits in a race car

commercial artist person who designs and illustrates things for other people

convertible car with a folding top

dashboard panel with gauges and controls in front of the driver of a car; also called a "dash"

drag race contest in which one car tries to go faster than another car in the shortest time possible

fender frame over the wheel of a car that protects the wheel and prevents splashing

formula exact specifications for size and weight of an open-wheel race car

grille open screen that covers the front part of a car

HUMVEE High Mobility Multipurpose Wheeled Vehicle

insignia badge or distinguishing mark

logo symbol, name, or trademark of a company

NASCAR National Association for Stock Car Auto Racing; organization that regulates stock car racing in the United States

roadster open automobile with a single seat

roll bar heavy, overhead metal bar on a vehicle that protects passengers if the vehicle turns over

spoiler fin or blade on the front or rear of a car that changes the airflow around the car and makes the car hold the road better at high speeds

straightedge wood, metal, or plastic bar used as a guide to draw straight lines

tread grooved part of a tire that presses against the ground

wheel well part of the body of a car that goes around the wheels

Art Glossary

crosshatching
marking that uses lines that cross each other

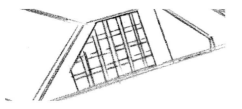

guideline
light line, used to shape a drawing, that is usually erased in the final drawing.

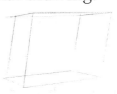

horizontal
line that is level or flat

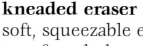

kneaded eraser
soft, squeezable eraser used to soften dark pencil lines

parallel
straight lines that lie next to one another but never touch

shade
make darker than the rest

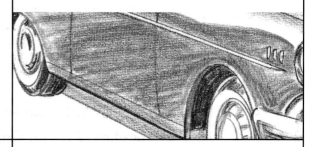

sketch
draw quickly and roughly

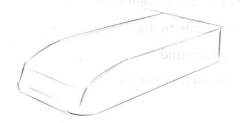

vertical
line that is straight up and down

More Books

Books about Drawing

Ames, Lee J. *Draw 50 Cars, Trucks, and Motorcycles.* Madison, Wis.: Demco Media, 1986.

Roberts, Michelle. *How to Draw Cars & Trucks & Other Vehicles.* Mineola, N.Y.: Dover Publications, Inc., 1999.

Tallarico, Tony. *I Can Draw Cars, Trucks, Trains, and Other Wheels.* New York, Simon and Schuster Childrens, 1997.

Books about Cars

Armentrout, Patricia. *Extreme Machines. . .On Land.* Vero Beach, Fla.: Rourke Press, Inc., 1998.

McKenna, A.T. *Corvette.* Minneapolis, Minn.: ABDO Publishing, 2000.

—. *Ferrari.* Minneapolis, Minn.: ABDO Publishing, 2000.

—. *Jaguar.* Minneapolis, Minn.: ABDO Publishing, 2000.

Index

Chevy Bel Air 8–9
classic car 8
convertible 8
Corvette 20–21
dragster 16–17
drawing
  advice 4
  tools 5, 31
dune buggy 18–19
Ford Model T 6–7
Formula One 12–13
Funny Car 14–15

Hummer 28–29
Jeep Grand Cherokee 24–25
NASCAR 10
Porsche Boxster 22–23
race car 10, 12, 14, 16, 18
stock car 10–11
Volkswagen Beetle 26–27